A HISTORY OF BRITAIN IN...

12

Assorted Animals

PAUL ROCKETT

W
FRANKLIN WATTS
LONDON•SYDNEY

Franklin Watts
Published in paperback in Great Britain in
2018 by The Watts Publishing Group

Editor: Sarah Peutrill
Design and illustration: Mark Ruffle
www.rufflebrothers.com

Dewey number: 590.9'41
ISBN: 978 1 4451 3612 7
Library ebook: 978 1 4451 3613 4

Printed in China

Franklin Watts
An imprint of
Hachette Children's Group
Part of The Watts Publishing Group
Carmelite House
50 Victoria Embankment
London EC4Y 0DZ

An Hachette UK Company
www.hachette.co.uk

www.franklinwatts.co.uk

CONTENTS

A NATION OF ANIMAL LOVERS

Today, Britain is known as a nation of animal lovers. More than 50% of British families own a pet and they spend around four billion pounds a year pampering them.

Britain was also the first country in the world to have a society that campaigned for animal welfare. However, animals have not always been so well-loved throughout the history of Britain.

Symbols of Britain

Animals have become symbols of countries around the world, and are seen to share the character of their nation.

British bulldog
The bulldog has become an emblem of Britain, symbolising the tough and determined character of the British people.

The British bulldog was first bred in England around the 16th century as an aggressive attack dog, used for sport.

Animals around Britain

British animals are protected in the wild, farmed for food and clothes and kept as pets.

Here are a few different animals from around the country.

Scottish terrier

Highland cow

Golden eagle

English springer spaniel

Manx cat

Puffin

Raven

Welsh mountain sheep

Bottlenose dolphin

Dartmoor pony

The following assorted animals...

The following pages provide an overview as to how animals have fared alongside the changing attitudes and events in British history. Whether loathed or loved, animals have played an important role in the history of Britain, through its sports, wars, royal favour and food production.

ANIMAL REMAINS

Animal bones and teeth found on archaeological sites help us learn about the interactions between people and animals in the past. Marks on bones, what they're buried alongside and how they're buried can tell us if the animal was farmed, hunted, slaughtered, eaten or worshipped.

Bones and coins

Animal bones that have knife marks scored on them tell us that the animal was butchered for meat. An animal buried with its skeleton still intact is likely to have been valued as a sacred creature.

Animals were also used as symbols. The horse was a popular emblem, associated with warriors and kings. Horses became an important animal during the Bronze Age (2500 BCE–800 BCE), when they were used to pull chariots.

During the Iron Age (800 BCE–43 CE), horses, along with stags and boars, appeared on jewellery, weapons and coins, representing wealth and strength.

The shapes on this Iron Age coin resemble a horse above a wheel, symbolising a war chariot. The coin was found in Lincolnshire and is from around the 1st century BCE.

1

The White Horse

On a hillside in Uffington, Oxfordshire, is a giant chalk carving of a horse, which dates back to the late Bronze Age, around 3,000 years ago. No one is entirely sure of its purpose; it can only be seen fully from the air, and so might have been created as a sign to the ancient gods. It was also built near a fort and so may have been the symbol of the tribe who lived there.

The White Horse at Uffington is 114 m long.

Animal facts

Around 5000–4500 BCE, the first farmers came over to Britain from mainland Europe, bringing with them cattle, sheep and goats.

Pigs were bred from boars (right) that roamed in the wild. Pet dogs were bred from wolves.

Some animals that lived off the coast of Scotland disappeared through changes in the weather and over-hunting. The walrus (above) vanished in 1000 BCE and the grey whale in 500 BCE.

IMPORTED ANIMALS

The Romans invaded Britain in 43 CE, adding Britain to an empire that covered parts of Europe, Africa and Asia. This large empire allowed the Romans to transport foreign goods between countries and introduce animals into places where they were previously unknown.

New animals

We can still see the descendants of many of the animals that the Romans brought to Britain. These include peacocks from Asia and dormice from south-east Europe. The dormice were bred for food, ensuring a steady supply of meat for the dinner table.

The Romans also brought over fallow deer from the Middle East, building game parks in which they could be hunted for sport.

Roman mosaic of a cat catching a bird

They introduced the domestic cat to Britain, popular for their rodent-catching skills around the home. They were kept to guard food stores against mice. The Roman army put cat symbols on their flags and shields.

Rabbit

2

Rabbits were brought over from Spain by the Romans. We know this, as the earliest evidence of rabbits in Britain are butchered rabbits' bones dating from 2,000 years ago. They were found amongst Roman pottery in Norfolk.

The Romans kept rabbits in walled enclosures and bred them for their meat and fur. It's likely that Britain's wild rabbits began with some who escaped. Today, there are approximately 45 million rabbits living wild in Britain.

Animal facts

The Roman army had a specially bred attack dog, similar to pit bull terriers, but now extinct. The Romans also had guard dogs and dogs they kept as pets. Some were used to keep their owner's bed warm, like a hot water bottle.

This is a statue of a Roman guard dog

The Roman period is also the time when rats began to arrive. Originally from Central Asia, they spread throughout Europe and arrived in Britain on ships.

Within the Roman Empire, animals were used for gruesome entertainment. People and animals, such as lions and leopards, fought each other to the death in amphitheatres. No one is certain whether these animals were used in Britain, as their remains have not been found. However, Chester's amphitheatre contains a block where animals or people were chained up before being released for combat.

FARM ANIMALS

The Anglo-Saxons came to Britain at around the time the Romans left. They were attracted by its rich land that was perfect for farming. They set up small farming communities in which animals were key to their survival – they provided meat for food and skins and wool for clothing.

Food and ink

Farm animals were much the same as today: sheep, pigs, cows and chickens. However, they were all much smaller in size, and the pigs were hairier and darker skinned.

Eggs from chickens were used for food but were also used by monks in the monasteries to mix with inks.

The egg whites were used to bind the colour pigment together, allowing manuscripts to have colourful illustrations.

Anglo-Saxon monks created this manuscript in the 11th century. It tells the story of Noah's Ark, with illustrations of farm animals at the bottom right.

3

Ox

The Anglo-Saxons also needed animals for farm work. Oxen were used in the fields. They pulled the plough, digging up the soil in which crop seeds were planted. The soil was often heavy and a ploughing team needed four to eight oxen to drag the plough through the earth.

This 11th century illustration shows a team of four oxen pulling a heavy plough. Keeping oxen was expensive and so they were shared amongst groups of farmers.

Animal facts

The month of January was known as 'wolf manoth', meaning wolf month. The Anglo-Saxons believed that people were more likely to be eaten by wolves during this month than at any other time. Also, the nobles hunted wolves between January and March.

Viking settlers, who arrived from the 7th century, also farmed sheep, pigs, cows and cattle. However they also milked their horses and ate horse meat – this was a practice forbidden by the Anglo-Saxon Christian Church.

Due to over-hunting, brown bears disappeared from Britain in around 1000 CE.

FOREST LAW

William the Conqueror came from Normandy, France. He fought an Anglo-Saxon ruler to become King of England in 1066. William was a great lover of hunting. He passed the Forest Law. This set aside large areas of land where only royalty and wealthy nobles could hunt.

The hunted

The Forest Law preserved much of Britain's wildlife. It protected animals so that they survived for the sport of hunting. These animals included deer, boars, hares and wolves.

All classes of people took part in hunting. However the Forest Law meant that only nobles could hunt these animals in certain areas of forest. Those caught poaching or chopping down trees within the protected areas faced imprisonment and large fines.

Hunting dogs and hawks were used to hunt animals, as shown in this scene from the Bayeux Tapestry.

Some of the forests that were preserved by William are still protected today, such as the New Forest in Hampshire.

4

Wolf

Wolves often roamed the countryside close to forests, terrorising villagers and farmers. The killing of wolves to protect livestock was encouraged. Nobles employed servants with the sole task of hunting wolves.

In 1281, King Edward I paid wolf hunters to kill as many wolves as they could. By the 15th century they had disappeared from the wild in England. They were hunted to extinction in Scotland in the late 1700s.

Animal facts

During Norman times, tormenting animals for entertainment became increasingly popular. Bears were imported for the purpose of bear baiting – a sport where animals, such as bulldogs, were set upon the bear, fighting each other to death. Bull baiting was also popular and special animal-baiting pits and rings were built.

Many of the words we use for animals and food come from the Norman French language of this period. These include our words for cow, beef, hen, pork and sheep.

The English word 'beef' comes from the Norman French word boeuf.

BIG BUSINESS

During medieval times, the wealth of England largely depended on one animal: the sheep. Their wool was exported throughout Europe, making huge sums of money for those that owned the farmland and for the king who placed a high tax on its export.

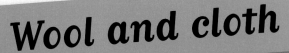

Wool and cloth

Cloth manufacturing became a big business. Teams of men and boys wove alongside each other in large workshops.

Women were able to make money from wool, spinning and weaving cloth in their homes.

This illustration, from 1340, shows a woman spinning yarn. The women who carried out this work were mainly unmarried and were called 'spinsters' – a name still associated with unmarried women today.

The excellent quality and quantity of wool that came from England was partly due to the wet climate. It provided long seasons with lush grass on which the sheep grazed. This helped their wool grow longer and fuller than sheep elsewhere.

This is a modern-day ball of Worsted wool yarn, named after the village of Worsted in Norfolk. Worsted wool was highly prized and popular across Europe, as it made cloth that was smooth and hard-wearing.

5

Cotswold sheep

The main centres of wool production were the Cotswolds, East Anglia, Lincolnshire and the Welsh borders. Each area became famous for its own breed of sheep.

The Cotswold sheep is good for wool as it grows a very thick fleece. It's also able to graze in different landscapes and can cope in harsh and hilly conditions.

The Cotswold sheep is known as a 'dual-use breed' as it is bred for both its wool and meat.

Animal facts

The Black Death struck Britain in 1348. This was a disease that killed millions. It was carried by fleas that lived upon black rats that arrived in Britain on merchant ships.

Flea

The white hart became the symbol of King Richard II, who ruled England from 1377–1399. It is now the fifth most popular name for a British pub.

'Hart' is another name for a stag.

In 1204, King John I established the royal menagerie in the Tower of London. It housed exotic animals given as gifts from abroad, such as lions, an elephant, monkeys and a polar bear that went out on a lead to hunt for fish in the Thames.

HEDGEHOG BOUNTY

In 1532, the Tudor king, Henry VIII, passed a law that encouraged everyone to hunt animals that roamed freely around the country. A bounty was placed on a list of vermin – creatures that were thought to be responsible for food shortages and for spreading disease.

Vermin

The list of vermin included:

hedgehogs
water voles
badgers
foxes
kites
ravens
woodpeckers
kingfishers
polecats
wild cats
stoats
weasels.

Rats were a huge problem in villages and towns, and being a rat catcher was a full-time job. This illustration shows a rat catcher advertising his trade.

A lot of money could be made from killing these creatures. Presenting the head of a badger or fox as proof of kill earned you three times more money than a day's work on a farm.

The Tudors were more concerned with the animals they kept for companionship, sport and food than those that lived in the wild. As a result, they hunted many of England's native species close to extinction. Before, wild animals were a common sight in the countryside. Even now many are rare to spot.

Hedgehog

6

Hedgehogs were considered a prime pest during Tudor times. People believed, wrongly, that they sucked the milk from cows as they lay down at night. Because of this, the hedgehog bounty was fairly high – four pennies – four times that of the polecat, wild cat, stoat and weasel.

The hunting of hedgehogs was so successful that it is thought to have brought them close to extinction.

The hedgehog still struggles to survive and there are fewer than one million in Britain today. However, it is much more popular than it was in Tudor times. In 2013, it was voted by the readers of BBC Wildlife Magazine *as Britain's national species.*

Animal facts

Monkeys were popular pets for royalty appearing in some of their portraits.

Portrait of Queen Catherine of Aragon (1485–1536) with her pet monkey.

Cats were seen by many as a symbol of the devil. During her coronation, Queen Elizabeth I (1533–1603) had a cat burned in a wicker basket to symbolise the releasing of demons.

WITCHCRAFT AND WAR

During the middle of the 17th century, a series of witch hunts took place, with women being accused of using magic to harm others. Witches were thought to have guides from the spirit world that took the shape of animals with supernatural powers.

Familiars

The animals that witches kept were known as 'familiars'. Dogs and cats were the most common familiars. Other familiars included animals associated with dirt, such as mice and toads, spreading disease as part of their magical powers.

This illustration from The Discovery of Witches *(1647), shows witches identifying their familiars in the shapes of a white kitten, a fat spaniel, a horned greyhound, a black rabbit and a polecat.*

The craze for witch hunts took place during the English Civil War (1642–51), when the country was divided in battle. Witches and familiars didn't really exist. They were created as scapegoats for the problems of this time and were linked to the enemy that was being fought.

7

Dog-witch

Charles I's nephew, Prince Rupert, fought in the English Civil War with his trusted pet poodle, Boye. His Royalist enemies accused Rupert of possessing dark magical powers and said that his poodle was the devil in disguise. Boye gained celebrity status as a dog-witch, with rumours that he could catch bullets in his mouth and predict the future.

This drawing is from a pamphlet called 'The Cruel Practices of Prince Rupert' (1643), showing Rupert and his dog Boye heading into battle.

Animal facts

Oliver Cromwell's government passed laws in England against the cruel sports of cock fighting and bull baiting. These were later overturned.

King Charles II (1630–1685) is associated with a small dog named after him – the King Charles Spaniel. Charles allowed his spaniels to roam freely around the palace and played with them during important meetings. His fondness for the dogs made them popular pets.

EXOTIC ANIMALS

During the 18th century, Britain's empire continued to expand across the world, introducing new and exotic creatures to the people of Britain. Strange new animals appeared in exhibitions and markets, becoming objects of curiosity and fashion.

Exhibits

Exotic animals were exhibited in city coffee shops. Here you could come for a drink and see rattlesnakes from North America and crocodiles from Africa.

Owning exotic animals was a sign of great wealth and refinement. Queen Charlotte (1744–1818) kept zebras in the royal stables, and her son, George (1762–1830), had pet electric eels.

Little was known about how to look after these foreign animals, and so many died not long after their arrival. Their remains were often stuffed and put on show, or used as decoration for ladies' fashions.

This illustration from 1774 shows visitors to a menagerie. A monkey (top left) is dressed as one of the fashionable visitors.

8

Kangaroo

Animal facts

From 1788, Britain began building colonies across Australia, encountering new animals such as the duck-billed platypus and the kangaroo.

The kangaroo became a symbol of British superiority and greatness – Britain had discovered a new creature unknown to the rest of Europe. For a while Britain was gripped with kangaroo mania, and its image appeared on decorative boxes, books and engravings. There was even a ship called HMS *Kangaroo*.

The first animal welfare law was passed in 1822, forbidding the 'cruel and improper use of cattle'.

The world's first scientific zoo, the London Zoo, opened in 1828. Many of the animals kept at the Tower of London (see page 15) ended up here.

Methods of taxidermy – stuffing dead animals – improved and stuffed animals became popular ornaments.

A stuffed black-and-white ruffed lemur from a collection kept in Westminster Library, London.

Kangaroos were kept at Kew, London, where they could roam freely on the banks of the Thames.

The SPCA (Society for the Prevention of Cruelty to Animals) was founded in a London coffee shop in 1824. It became the RSPCA in 1840.

HARD LABOUR

Coal was the main source of energy in Victorian times. It was used for powering factory machines, steamships and locomotives. Coal is buried in rocks deep beneath the ground, and children and ponies were used to move heavy cartloads of coal along dark underground shafts.

Children and animals

Working in coal mines came with the risk of being trapped by collapsing shafts, poisoned by gases or being blown up by explosions.

In 1842 a law was passed to stop children under the age of ten from working in mines, and in 1874 the age was raised to fourteen. To replace child labour, more horses and ponies were used and by 1913 an estimated 70,000 pit ponies were working in Britain.

This illustration shows the work that children did in the coal mines. It was printed in the government report on children in mining in 1842.

Victorian pit pony. Many ponies were born in underground stables, never seeing sunlight.

Pit pony

Animal facts

Pit ponies were suitable for working underground in mines because of the following features:

Size: *small for low, narrow spaces*
Strength: *strong enough to pull several loads of coal at once and work long hours*
Hardiness: *able to cope with harsh underground conditions*
Intelligence: *could be trained easily.*

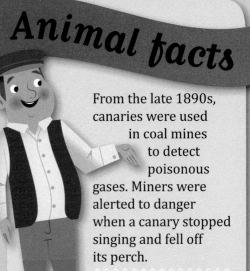

From the late 1890s, canaries were used in coal mines to detect poisonous gases. Miners were alerted to danger when a canary stopped singing and fell off its perch.

Although many animal rights groups protested at the use of pit ponies, they continued to work underground up until 1999, when most of Britain's coal mines had closed.

A common breed for a pit pony was the Shetland pony.

Grey squirrels were imported from North America in the mid-19th century, and quickly came to dominate British woodlands.

The SPB (Society for the Protection of Birds) was founded in 1889. It was formed as a response to the trade in exotic feathers that were plucked for use in women's hats. It became the RSPB in 1904.

In 1859, Charles Darwin published a controversial book, *On the Origin of Species*. Most people believed that God had created all living things, whereas Darwin claimed that animals evolved over generations, adapting for survival. His book had a big influence on attitudes towards animals.

Victorian fashions featured large plumage on women's hats.

ANIMALS AT WAR

During the First and Second World Wars (1914–18; 1939–45) animals were used for the war effort at home and abroad.

Animal employment

During the First World War, horses were used in cavalry regiments carrying soldiers into battle. Horses were also essential for transporting ammunition and pulling ambulances and guns.

In both the First and Second World Wars, trained dogs were used to sniff out mines, and search and dig out bomb victims – tasks that they are still used for in war today.

The Royal Scots Greys cavalry regiment in France, 1918

During the Second World War the Dickin Medal began to be awarded to animals that had shown a 'devotion to duty'. The medal was awarded to 53 animals, of which 32 were homing pigeons.

A soldier takes bandages from a British dog working for the Red Cross in the First World War.

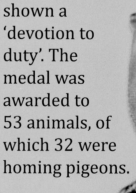
The Dickin Medal

Carrier pigeon

Animal facts

During the Second World War, the National Pigeon Service was formed. This was an organisation made up of 200,000 pigeons used to relay important messages that saved the lives of many British soldiers.

The pigeons flew for miles, often facing gunfire and attacks by hawks trained to kill them.

Messages were placed in special containers, either on their legs or, as seen in this photo, in small pouches over their backs.

Royal Air Force bombers carried pigeons to send messages if they crashed. This photo shows the carrier pigeon Winkie and the RAF crew who were rescued after he flew 193 km back to his base.

It's estimated that around eight million British horses, mules, camels and bullocks died in service during the First World War.

The first British guide dogs were trained to be used by survivors of the First World War. Guide Dogs for the Blind was later established in 1934.

The RSPCA set up 734 animal rescue centres during the Second World War. These were largely established to care for the casualties and stray animals affected by the Blitz.

Animals became popular mascots during both wars. These included Venus the bulldog (below), mascot of HMS *Vansittart* during the Second World War.

ANIMAL WELFARE

The second half of the 20th century saw Britain pass more laws to protect the welfare of animals than ever before. The well-being of animals became a big issue, especially in science, fashion and the food industry.

Fashion and animal testing

In the 1970s, attitudes to the use of animals in the fashion and cosmetics industries began to change. In 1976 The Body Shop started selling 'animal friendly' cosmetics that had not been tested on animals.

In the 1980s there were huge campaigns against the fur industry that made the wearing of fur unfashionable.

By the start of the 21st century, the testing of cosmetics on animals and the farming of animals for their fur had both been outlawed in Britain.

In 2009, The Body Shop received a Lifetime Achievement Award from the RSPCA for their commitment and support for animal welfare.

It takes up to 40 dumb animals to make a fur coat.

But only one to wear it.

LYNX

If you don't want animals gassed, electrocuted, trapped or strangled, don't buy a fur coat.

This poster, from 1985, was by the animal rights organisation Lynx. They used hard-hitting images to get their message across causing a huge drop in the sale of furs.

Battery hen

Post-war Britain saw an increase in the demand for cheap food on a large scale. This transformed the way many animals were farmed, from roaming in open fields to being contained in conditions like a factory production line.

Battery hens are kept in small, cramped cages. The hens' beaks and claws are trimmed so that they can't scratch and peck each other. They never leave their cages or see natural light.

Animal rights groups highlight cruel conditions like these, to encourage the public to shop differently and put pressure on governments to protect the welfare of animals.

Keeping battery hens, as shown in this picture, has been banned in Britain since 2012.

Animal facts

The world's first cloned animal, Dolly the sheep, was born in 1996. This was a breakthrough in science – creating another animal from a cell from an adult mammal.

It is hoped that the exploration of animal cloning will help find cures to human illnesses.

Dolly died in 2003. Her remains were stuffed for display.

In the late 1980s, 'mad cow disease' struck British cattle. This is an infection that harms the health of cattle and also their meat. As a result, millions of cattle were destroyed, and a ten-year ban was placed on British beef in Europe.

A popular cartoon in the 1980s, 'Teenage Mutant Ninja Turtles', led to an increase of red-eared terrapins as pets. Their number also increased in the wild, as many pet owners dumped them in lakes and rivers, or flushed them down the loo.

RETURN TO THE PAST

The 21st century has seen many efforts to reintroduce animals that were once native to Britain back into the wild. The hope is to protect species from extinction and restore balanced ecosystems that can survive without any interference from humans.

Reintroducing...

A small number of beavers have been reintroduced into Scotland. It's hoped they will benefit the surrounding wildlife by creating new habitats as well as prevent flooding by slowing the flow of water with the dams they build around their burrows.

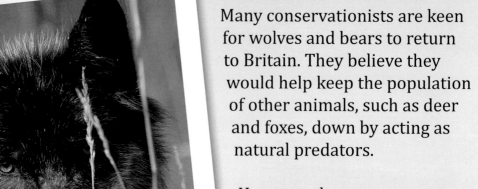

Many conservationists are keen for wolves and bears to return to Britain. They believe they would help keep the population of other animals, such as deer and foxes, down by acting as natural predators.

However, there are concerns about these creatures moving outside forests and woodlands, and possibly attacking people and livestock – as they did in the past.

Red kite

Animal facts

The red kite is a bird of prey whose fortunes have gone up and down throughout the history of Britain.

In the Middle Ages the red kite was protected by royal decree, being valued as a scavenger who helped clean the streets. However, during Tudor times it was placed on the 'vermin list' and was widely hunted for money.

Red kites are important to forest ecosystems. They keep down the number of small mammals by eating them.

By the 20th century only two pairs of red kites were known to exist in Britain. However, a successful programme of reintroduction has meant that there are now around 1,500 pairs of red kites living in Britain today.

The most popular pets in Britain in the 21st century are goldfish, cats and dogs.

There are approximately 18 million goldfish kept as pets in Britain.

There are around 7.7 million cats kept as pets in Britain.

There are around 6.6 million dogs kept as pets in Britain.

Further information

Books

Britannia: Great Stories from British History by Geraldine McCaughrean (Orion, 2014)

British Animals series (Wayland, 2012)

Nature Detectives: British Mammals by Victoria Munson (Wayland, 2013)

The Story of Britain by Mick Manning and Brita Granstrom (Franklin Watts, 2014)

Tracking Down series by Moira Butterfield (Franklin Watts, 2013)

Websites

BBC Nature website with photos and information to help you identify British wildlife:
www.bbc.co.uk/nature/places/United_Kingdom

RSPCA website with interactive resources on what the RSPCA does as well as giving tips on looking after animals and pets:
www.rspca-education.org.uk

Children's British History Encyclopedia featuring a timeline with detailed information from each era and information on finding and interpreting historical evidence:
history.parkfieldict.co.uk/

Why were some animals so important during the First World War? Find out here:
www.bbc.com/education/clips/zwc8jxs

Glossary

ammunition
objects, such as bullets and grenades, that are thrown or fired from a weapon in order to cause damage

amphitheatre
a circular building with rows of seats surrounding a space that is used for theatre performances or sports

archaeological site
a space where evidence of the past has been preserved

baiting
cruelly tormenting an animal, often done in the past as a form of entertainment

Blitz, the
period of German air raids on cities in Britain during the Second World War

bounty
an amount of money given as a reward for catching a criminal

conservationist
a person who works to preserve the natural environment

descendants
family relations, or animals that have developed from an earlier species in history

ecosystem
community of organisms interacting within an environment

emblem
an object, person or animal that is used to represent something else, such as a country

empire
a group of countries governed under a single authority, such as under one ruler or country

enclosure
a space that has been closed off for the use of farming or as private land

export
goods or services sold to another country

extinct
having no living members; a species that has died out

familiars
a spirit that usually takes the form of an animal and works as an assistant to a witch

livestock
farm animals that are bought, sold and reared for commercial reasons

menagerie
the place where a collection of animals are kept to be exhibited

Neolithic
early period of history, also known as the last stage of the Stone Age, when stone tools, pottery and farming developed

nobles
people that belong to a high social class, often having a title such as duke or baroness

poacher
someone who kills or takes wild animals illegally

predator
animal that kills other animals for its own survival

Royalist
a supporter of the royal family in the English Civil War

sacred
connected to a god or a religious purpose or ceremony

scapegoat
someone who takes the blame and is punished for acts of others

scavenger
person or animal that collects unwanted items, such as leftover food

shaft
a long narrow space providing access to a mine

species
living things that contain shared characteristics, e.g. human beings

vermin
wild animals that are believed to be harmful or carry diseases

Index